WEAVING

FOR

BEGINNERS

Make Your First Wire Jewelry Project and Learn Basic Wire Weaving Skills

Table of Contents

INTRODUCTION

Wire weaving is a basic part of wire jewelry making. It is a vital technique and skill useful for projects that have to do with art, creativity, and wires. Patterns, curls, and directions are essential in wire weaving and must be properly understood to have the best of wire weaving works. Therefore, in the scope of this book, the integral knowledge needed for beginners in the art of wire weaving is provided in simple and clear words with no ambiguity at all. With total belief, this knowledge gives all and sundry the opportunity to make their first jewelry even without close supervision but just by the help of this book. This book covers basic weaves like the Snake Weave, Flame Stitch and other two-wire weaves. Also, various techniques such as coiling, wrapping, weaving, turtle necking to mention but a few, will be discussed. Three practical projects will be taught too with basic knowledge on how to make and install clasps, how to polish and wax the wires, how to splice and alongside incorporate beads into your designs. Helpful tips and links for better research and study are provided in the book with a chart on metric conversion. This book is amazingly perfect for beginners and can be used by experts too. It has been designed in a practical way; get the equipment needed and make your first wire weavings.

TOOLS

Here is a brief list of tools you will require:

1. Chain nose plier
2. Flat nose plier
3. Pointy flush cutter
4. Wires (of different types, lengths, diameters, sizes, and metals)
5. Clasps

DEFINITION OF TERMS

1. Weaving wire: Otherwise called warp wire/ adds-on wire. It is used to make the necessary movement when necessary. In most times it's very flexible and soft for wrapping around the base wire.

2. Base wire: This is the foundation of any wire works. It is very strong to withstand the rigorous movement of the warp wire. It is flexible but strong. It determines the shape and structure of the whole jewelry.

WEAVES AND TECHNIQUES

WEAVES

Two wire weaves

These two wire weaves are basic weaving styles and are also referred to as "wraparounds." This is to describe how the base wires are held together by wrapping weaving wires around them. Let's consider two weaves that employ the use of two wires.

Weave 1: The basic figure eight weave

For this weave, you will need two base wires (16, 18 or 20 gauge) with a particular length, which depends on how big your project is and a smaller gauge, though longer wire for wrapping.

Steps

1. Hold the two base wires, at the desired distance, in your left hand and wrap your weaving wire around the top base wire a couple of times using your right hand. This is

to attach your weaving wire to the base wire and give it a firm hold.

2. Wrap around each consecutively. I am going up and around the first base wire, down and between the two base wires then up, over and around the second base wire likewise.

This weave should produce a shape that looks like figure Eight around the bare wires. Repeat these steps until your desired length is reached.

Weave 2: Double Coils

This weave is similar to the basic figure eight weave. A slight change in the pattern is a double wrap around each of the two base wires before moving to the next. Just as indicated in the basic eight-figure weave, two base wires and a smaller weaving wire are needed.

Steps

1. Hold the two base wires at the desired distance in your left hand and wrap your weaving wire around the top base wire a

couple of times using your right hand. This is to attach your weaving wire to the base wire and give it a firm hold.

2. Now wrap your weaving wire on the top base wire two times and then move between the two base wires to wrap the other base wire twice too.

Note that

1. The upper end of the base wires far above your right hand should be left open to allow you to weave between and around the wires comfortably.

2. To get good tension, pull the weave wire closely around the warp/base wire to form fine lines and for the weaving wires to really take the shape of the base wires.

3. After repeating the patterns, directions and flow couple of times, scoot them together if you find any weird space using your finger or

nails. Do not use a tool to do this because you can knick up the wire.

4. Be careful not just to pull the weave wire around the base wire, leave it loose and try to tug, tug and tug until it tightens. This is because you are most likely going to get a kink or it will leave it with a lot of slack that will alter the weave. Instead, bring the wire all the way around the wire to which you want it on. All the way around, between and closely. Make sure that you are placing it where it is really ought to be craftily while bending it to the expected position.

5. For practice, improvise by using slightly thick copper wires for the base and any soft wire or copper too for weaving.

6. The number of wraps around each base wire is not limited to just one or two. A consistent number of your choice in one design can be employed. Creativity is highly permitted though it must be done in symmetry, so it makes sense.

SNAKE WEAVE

The snake weave is a three wire weave that employs the use of three base wires of about 1 millimeter each and a weaving wire of any length. It is advisable to start with three feet for your weaving wire; this is because it is hard to weave when it's more than that. You can add more when you run out. This technique that involves ending a wire and adding another (splicing) is also discussed later in this book.

Steps

1. Attach the weaving wire to one of the base wires. Place another of the base wire, just above the first one and on top of the weaving wire. Then wrap around both wires twice just as if you have one base wire and return to the position below the two base wires.
2. Now bring the third base wire and lay it above the rest of the base wires and on top of the weaving wire.

3. Pull the weaving wire from behind the new base wire upwards and in between the first two base wires.

   If you take the two wires and wrap both at the same time, there will be complete overlap of the wires, and this would not be able to get your weave wired up and coiled into the next direction.

4. Now wrap around the bottom two base wires twice again. Then push them all the way down with your fingers or nails gently.

5. Repeat these steps over and over till you have perfected the weave style or have met the expected length.

FLAME STITCH

This flame stitch looks like a weave with two sections looking different but are actually the same pattern of the basic weave. The only difference is that at the start of the weave, the weaves are tightly packed and barely spaced whereas the other section is well and nicely spaced with equal intervals and spaces. For this weave style, you will need five(5) base wires of about 1 mm and 18 gauge each and a length of 0.4mm round wire of about 26 gauge.

Steps

The closely packed section comes first

1. Grab one of your base wires and attach your weaving wire against the base wire just by wrapping a couple of times. Push the curls neatly together.
2. Add another base wire to expand the weave by placing it above the previous base wire and make the weaving wire come out between the two at the back. Then bring the base wire around the bottom base wire then over against both of the base wires towards the back.
3. Add another base wire (the third one as at now). This wire will be on the top of the other base wires horizontally. The weaving wire is coming out from between the top two base

wires (i.e., between the 2nd and 3rd; the newly added base wire).

4. Move the weaving wire between the two that you just wrapped (i.e., between the 1st and 2nd base wires). Push this all down and keep the distance and closeness constant. Then go all the way over the top two base wires and wrap around them.

5. After this, allow the weaving wire to go all the way down through the third base wire and over the two at the bottom (The same that were wrapped together at first). Allow the weaving wire to go down between the top two base wires.

6. The next base wire is placed, unlike the former ones, below the others and on top of the weaving wire. The weaving wire then goes all the way behind the base wires and over the top two bottom base wires so that the new wire is included. Now the weaving wire is between the 2nd and 3rd bottom base wires at the back.

7. The fifth and last base wire is now added at the bottom below all others, like the recent former base wire. The weaving wire comes behind all the base wires from the 2nd bottom base wire and over the top of the bottom two base wires, so the new one is included. Always remember to push the wavy pattern all the way down to keep it close and neat. The weaving wire is now between the now 2nd and 3rd base wires

8. From behind the 3rd out of the five base wires, come in between the two you just wrapped up (i.e., between the 1st and 2nd bottom base wires), to return to the middle base wires in order to perform the same wavy weaves on the other side. Move the weaving wire upward over the next two base wires and down between the 3rd and 4th base wires. From behind, go between the two base wires you just wrapped together.

9. Go over the next two base wires (i.e., the 4th and 5th), then move down behind three base

wires going back to the middle base wire. Here the weaving wire is between the 2nd and 3rd base wires.

10. Once more, move over the two base wires going upwards and down between the 4th and 5th base wires.

11. Again, move the weaving wire up over the next two base wires so that the weaving wire is between the 3rd and 4th base wires and down behind the 4th base wire. You can then move the weaving wire up between the two you just wrapped (i.e., the weaving wire will be found between the 3rd and 4th base wires).

12. From the current location of the weaving wire, move down again under all the base wires and over the top of the two at the bottom, so it is stationed in between the 2nd and 3rd base wires, and between the two you just wrapped. After that, move over the next two including the middle base wire, so your weaving wire is between the 3rd and 4th base wire.

The spaced section of the flame stitch is just as indicated for the first section but rather more spaced.

Steps

1. After you must have repeated the patterns of the first section explained above severally, finish your curl and allow the weaving wire to be just behind the middle base wire; having two at the top and three below. So the weaving wire is between the 3rd and 4th base wire.

2. Wrap the weaving wire around the middle base wire a couple of times, this is dependent on you and how far apart you want them to be. For example, use three wraps.

3. The weaving wire should be just between and below the 3rd and 4th base wire. The same pattern as explained in the first section is what you do here too, but the spacing (that is,

the three wraps around the middle base wire at intervals) is what makes the difference.

4. The wire comes from behind the middle wire, and over the next two wires and up between the two you just wrapped. It then goes over the top of the next two base wires, down behind them and again up below the middle wire.

5. Before you go to the next side, wrap around the middle base wire three times, as proposed and just as you started. Then move down over the next two base wires which are above the middle base wire. This places the weaving wire in between the 3rd and 4th base wires, down behind and all the way over the top of the bottom two.

6. Finally, come up between the two base wires you just wrapped and push it down and over the next two base wires just above the middle wire. Also, put it between the 3rd and 4th base wires and go through the spacing again(the three wraps around the middle base wire)

Lastly, repeat the weaves until your desired length is attained.

TECHNIQUES

COILING

In wire weaving and jewelry making, coiling is a basic and essential technique that should be learned and incorporated. Coiling is an easy wire working technique and would be explicitly explained in this section. Coiling involves using a weaving wire around a base wire in the form of a helix. It is advised that you practice this wire weaving technique with brass or copper wire before you get to perfection.

For this technique you'll need:

5 inches length of 16 gauge base wire

2 feet of 18 gauge weaving/wrapping wire

Ruler or Tape rule

Marker

Chain/flat nose plier

Pointy flush cutter

Steps

1. Using the Pointy flush cutter, cut 5 inches length of 16 gauge wire for your base wire and 2 feet length of 18 gauge wire for your weaving wire after marking these lengths using your ruler. Mark out, at both ends, 1inch on your 5 inches base wire using your marker.

2. Use your flat nose plier to grasp the end of the weaving wire and bend it to about 45 degrees towards yourself. This serves as a tail that gives the weaving wire a better grip for coiling.

3. Using your left (non-dominant) hand, hold the tail end of the wire between your index finger and your thumb and slide the base wire into the bent space of the weaving wire.

4. Starting from the 1inch marked point on your base wire, use your plier to squeeze gently the bent weaving wire against the base wire.

Push outwards and downwards the weaving wire to begin the coils around the base wire.

5. Keep the coils running around the base wire repeatedly till you have reached the other 1inch mark. Use your Pointy flush cutter to cut the excess weaving wire away. To tidy things up, use your chain nose plier to tuck each end of the weaving wire in.

And you're done! Your coiled wire is ready.

WRAPPING

In the auspices of expounding and learning wire weaving skill, wrapping is a technique that requires using wire. It teaches how to wrap around a loop. This loop helps you attach this piece with other wire loops to make a necklace and/or bracelet.

For this technique, you will need:

Just a wire; the base wire

Round nose pliers

Pointy flush Cutters

Ruler

Steps

1. The very first thing to do is to measure and cut the wire (of your desired length, let's say 6inches) for usage. Make sure it is straight and not rumpled.

2. Using your dominant hand, take up your plier, and make a 90degree bend at a marked point of 2.5 inches from the end of the wire. Thereafter, twist the bent wire backward using your round nose plier, the tail should be hanging down!

3. Make sure to hold your round nose plier in your dominant hand with the bent wire pointing towards you from between the pliers. You can now bend the end of the short wire back using the thumb of your nondominant hand. And with plier, bend the shorter end of the wire around the other end.

4. Now remove the plier from the semi-circle loop you just made, reinsert the plier and twist the loop, reassembling it to form a perfect circle.

5. Hold onto the loop gently using your plier to prevent plier marks on it. Using your fingers, wrap the end of the wire around the stem of the loop tightly.

6. With about three to four rounds around the loop, you have made a great example of the wrapping technique. Cut out, cautiously, the excess short wire using your pointy flush cutter and avoid a sharp edge.

SPLICING

Splicing is a very simple technique basically created through a loop and at least three wires. Very many workers employ splicing, but it is basic and unique to wire works. The goal is to create a kind of hair-plaited look; thus, the need to have three wires crossed together which are held at the loop end with a plier. It is advisable to use soft and flexible wire for a beginner alongside handkerchief to hold the wires to avoid bruise. Most importantly, splicing is used in joining wires together; a process no wire weaving expert could elude while creating jewelry.

Splicing requires the following equipment:

6" to 3" Wires cut; the base and working

Round nose pliers

Chain nose pliers

A wire gauge

Steps

1. The first thing to do is to gauge how long you want the wire to be which should be based on the kind of jewelry to be made.

2. Then, pick the wires and make a cut of 2 and half of 16 or 18-inch gauge of the wires. Pick up your round nose pliers, make a loop and use it to hold the loop relative tight. You have to be careful with the manner the wire will be turning around the plier, hold it firmly and avoid movement whatsoever.

3. After you have got stability, push the wire at the extreme towards the loop you are holding and coil —the coiling process was the first technique to be explained, revise it, if need be.

4. After the coil, move the pliers to it and push the working wire (the major wire you are using to the coil) to make a continuous coil until you've gone round with enough.

5. At this point, hold the wires with your hand and remove the pliers to make a quick bend and continue with the coiling, make it halfway through.

6. With the bend, you have made a demarcation which will guide you. Use the round nose pliers to the grasp the wire in the about ¼ way along with the coil, then push the ends towards the jaw.

7. Then, you will need to make a finch end of the wires through the chain nose pliers. To do this, make an upward but tiny bend at the tip end of the hook using the pliers.

8. Move the loop towards the jewelry and use the rubber mallet to hit it.

    Make sure you repeat processes until the desired result is got. Alas, your splicing is very much ready!

GOOSENECK HOOK

This kind of technique of more or less like an addition to a primary design. This is because gooseneck hook is basically used in bracelet and necklace which are designed using other techniques. As important as starting jewelry is, finishing it up with gooseneck hook is one of the things any designer can't elude, even you. Gooseneck serves as connecting link with air in jewelry designing. Note that, this hook will add about a quarter inch to your length and thus proper considerations must be given to it.

Coming up with a good gooseneck hook technique, the following are the basic equipment for a workable gooseneck hook:

Wires 16 to 18 gauge

Round nose pliers

Chain nose pliers

Hammer

Steps

1. Since it is more or less addition to works, the first thing to do is to create a loop using the sharp end of your pliers.
2. Hold tight the loop and push the tail end of the wire towards it, start making a coil.
3. With this, a new part must've been created, move the pliers from the loop to the new part and hold the wire for continuous coiling until it moves about the loop.
4. After creating the coil, you will need to create a bend using the round nose pliers and continue with the wire movement around the coil in about halfway distance.

5. After enough coiling, use the more significant part of the round nose pliers hold the active wire and push it to the jaw. Make sure you observe about one-quarter distance away from the coil.

6. To the chain nose pliers, remember the round nose is still holding the wire, drag the wire till you get a tiny tip, make a bend and pinch it. Slip the hook now towards a piece of jewelry.

7. Lastly, depending on the wires used; 16 or 18 gauges; hit the hook slightly until a smooth is reached.

CRISS-CROSS FINISHED ENDS

This technique is like a finished cleaning means of keeping and tucking every end of the wires used in production. Of course when you create pieces of jewelry, many of the wires, both base and working, might be remaining at the tail end. These tail end will, in order to make the work neat, need to be kept –the process of maximizing this is crisscross finished ends. With this technique, tapping don the bracelet in order to create a loop for the clasp is done in a simple way. There are different sizes of wires to be used in this technique but start with 16 base alongside 8 and 9 add-on wires. You will need to get the 16 gauge as the base then pull the 8 gauge to the left end side while the 9 to the extreme left side crossed over the 8 gauge. With this first adjustment, all the wires are to be used as the base. These gauges aren't strictly used; you can choose to do it with another gauge but be sure every step meets the expected ends.

To make great crisscrossed ends, the following are what would be needed:

Wires in 16, 20, 8, 9, 15, etc. gauges

14 and 20 framing wires

Chain nose pliers

Round nose pliers

Nylon-jaw pliers

3. Pick your 24 gauge adds-on wire and make a cut of about 3 inches on it.

4. Pick the thread and thrust it through the loop created by the T-pin. Make sure you wrap the wire end twice and cut or trim the tips.

5. After then, through the right side beside the base wires, bring the add-on wires from the back end and attach a bead to it. Make sure when you're pushing the wires that they are towards the weave created.

6. You will need to balance the position of the wires, so pick the adds-on wire in between the base wire and make sure it is at the center. To ensure everything is tight, pull the base and add-on wires.

7. Like you did with bring the adds-on wire to the center through the base wires from the back, bring the wire again near the beads and make sure every space is guided firmly.

8. When you have got the adds-on wires close to the beads, wrap them about two hundred and twelve times around the beads and make

sure you pull the wire tight through the beads.

9. Do you remember that your T-pin that started the work is right there? Fine, bring the wire through the same direction you started with. Be extremely careful as the wire will want to shrink and rip off even from the loop; control this by hold from the loop your wires with holder, perhaps wires.

10. Lastly, remove the holder from the loop, straight the wires smoothly with round nose pliers and your work is ready.

Note that handling the wires firmly, especially the base wires, with your steady hand and move the adds-on wires with the weak one as this process could be a bit tedious without proper monitoring. For a start, ensure you repeat the process whenever you get stocked or move without getting the desired goals. You can start off, after the first step, to use the holder in order to have everything intact to avoid any form of frustrations through repeated getting of undesired and deserved results. Be extremely careful but creative.

PROJECTS

WOVEN LINK NECKLACE

To work out a project, be prepared to 'waste' materials and repeat the same thing at different times. The heart of this work is based on the first half of the Flame Stitch weave. These wire works are one of the most basic that used the techniques discussed. This work is a necklace weaved together. It is gorgeous and adjustable. This necklace is adjoined with turquoise seed beads. With a spiral technique, individual woven links are joined together. You must give yourself to much practice till the uphill pattern is formed. You must be prepared to start the work and finish on the spot, at least as a beginner.

Techniques for the woven link necklace are:

Weaving

Wrapping

Spiral

Goose necking

Cutting of wires

Therefore, revise the technique at a glance and do as instructed. You have to inculcate neatness in your work from the beginning.

To do this beginner project, you will need the following materials:

32 in. 18-gauge dead soft copper wire

80 in. 20-gauge dead soft copper wire

15 ft. 24-gauge dead-soft copper wire

11 to 60 Turquoise seed beads

Chain nose pliers

Flush cutter

The step by step guide, to be followed strictly:

Step 1

You will need to create the base of woven first. For the base wire of the woven link, pick the 20 gauge wire and cut four, of 4-inches, pieces of 20-gauge wire.

Step 2

Then for the weaving, cut a 3-ft. piece of 24-gauge wire to be used straightened before weaving, though.

Step 3

Complete the Uphill Wire Preparation, double wrap for the Flame Stitch with four base wires.

Step 4

Afterward, start with the first base wire by bringing the weaving wire straight down and working on the uphill portion of the Flame Stitch.

Step 5

Then double wrap the wires at this point. Make sure everything is intact and not loosened.

Step 6

Gradually, as you reach the top of each hill, move downwards, just behind the current place you are, with the weaving wire, and go directly into the uphill weave on the base wire again.

Step 7

Repeat the weave until you have woven 2 inches. You must be using the ruler at this point to monitor the progress of the weave.

Step 8

You will need to center the weave, now, pull each base wire outward with chain nose pliers. Because of the way you have been weaving, notice that the ends of the wires are not equal and trim the ends so you have one-quarter inches of wire on every side.

Step 9

Using three-step pliers, grasp all four wires on end at the same time and roll them inward for medium-sized loops.

Step 10

Leave the loops open so you can slide the connector in place later. Do this on both ends to finish your first woven link.

Step 11

The work is almost ready, and you have just laid a good foundation for your work. For the complete work, you will need more than two wovens. Therefore to get up to five woven links, repeat steps six and seven. Put them in another place; you will know where to join them later.

Step 12

Because you have five woven links, make five Spiral Connectors, a Gooseneck Hook, and a tip for your extension chain.

Step 13

You must have got the last shape of the work. With the spiral connectors connect together all the pieces from the beginning. Likewise, the loops should be connected to the ends of the woven links. Join all five of the woven links as well.

Step 14

Pick the chain nose pliers and tighten each loop around the spiral connector.

In order to let the necklace fit, customize by laying it down and massage with the mallet. Be careful not break beads sandwiched therein.

Your necklace is ready, flaunt it to impress people. CHUCKLES!

WOVEN EARRINGS

To make a stunning look, for a lady, put on a pair of simple but sophisticating earrings. These earrings are made with and display a pair of vibrant stones. Among all things to do first, you must first weave, in a single wrap, the base wire in order to frame up your Flame Stich's patterns. This weave must be four in number for energetic downhill patterns.

The techniques to employ for this project include:

Weaving

Wrapping

Crisscross

The materials are:

Pair of decorative earring

32 in. 20-gauge dead-soft sterling-silver wire

Chain nose pliers

20 in. 26-gauge dead-soft sterling-silver wire

Flame stitch

4 ft. 24-gauge dead-soft sterling-silver wire

2 to 3mm round sterling silver beads

2 to 10x15mm amethyst cabochons

Cutter

Ruler

The step by-step-guide:

Follow the steps below strictly and observe the change you make at every point:

Step 1 (cutting)

You're starting with your 20 gauge wire for the base. On the wire, cut four 4-in. pieces and make sure you check whether their sizes are equal. Drop this.

Pick your 24-gauge wire that will be used for waving and make a cut of 2-ft. pieces.

Step 2

Because you'll need to complete the uphill wire planning and arrangement, with your base wire (20-gauge), make a single wrap with all the four base wires. Drop this.

Step 3

Measure 1 inch of flame stitch. From the downhill to the uphill pattern making, weave alternately, the downhill to the uphill. To know whether you have completed a hill, weave one uphill and one downhill weaving pattern consecutively.

Step 4

You will make a full 14 hills that are one-inch long weave pattern. Make sure —through pulling every base wire using the chain nose pliers —every of your weave is center on the base wires.

Step 5

At this point, you'll have to make sure there is about 1 1/2 in. of a weave on the sides; both base and working wires. Make sure the weaves are tightly held together to avoid scattering.

Step 6

Once you attained stability, pick up your stones. Then, make a U-shape, bend the weave that is close to the curve of one end of your stone. Note that the shape you've carved doesn't have to be perfect, but a little smaller than the stone itself. At the top, crisscross the base wires, alternating left and right.

Step 7

Back to the base wires, pull all the four wires downwards equally and placed within the same spacing.

Step 8

Then, with your index finger and thumb on the left, hold the sixth wire tightly and bend the first base wire over it like a crisscross. Total carefulness needs to be taken here as you pull the wires and cross them on one another –you must maintain the shape throughout. While you are moving around the stones, ensure that the grip on the sixth base wire isn't jeopardized. Do this again and again.

Step 9

After the moving of base wires, turn the weave to the other side and trim the first base wire to about 3/8 inches.

Step 10

With the chain nose pliers, make a single and loose wrap of base wire one and six. Perhaps you label the wires for easy identification. Put the wire in their right proportion and don't let them stiff. Note that the best thing to do is to start with this loose wrapping and locking of each base because it makes the work easier and gives it the desired, don't forget to keep the shape all the time.

Step 11

It is time to insert the stone. Make sure the weave you have created is relatively small so that the stone will fit in very well —which is the bezel —trim the loops and tight them.

Step 12

That part is ready, and you will need to do the same thing for the other base wires to make sure the direction of movement is inward and held tight together during the wraps making.

Step 13

When you are done, at the top of everything, make a wrap and hold the intersected area with the chain nose. Make sure you trim the left side sixth base wire.

Put in a 3mm bead on the 6th base wire and make a double wrapped weave just above the bead while making a connection to the earring before the wrap is complete.

Using your pointy flush cutter, trim the wrap closely on the back.
Strap the stone into the bezel.

Cut a 10 inches piece of 26 gauge wire; this you will use to wrap the left side of the weave, towards the end. Wrap this wire around the weave about 5-6 times, then to the right, next to where the crisscross section begins. Trim the end close on the back.

Now crisscross the stone like you are lacing up your shoe using the 26 gauge wire. Go backward and forward five times. Wrap around the 6th base wire using the 26-gauge wire three times to the crisscross section so as to replicate the wrap made before. Trim the end closely and neatly on the back. Make the second earring to make a pair. Create a finish with liver of sulfur and buff.

DONUT BAIL PENDANT

This is very simple work and thus requires simple skill. Because of its end product, which is a whole donut bail pendant, there will be a preparative work prior to the main job. In other words, this project is a beginner one but combines simple preparatory works with the main one. The preparation is expedient because without it the foundation will not be made for the huge job. In the same vein, the main job needs a pendant so, make sure the size and type of the pendant are determined too. Make sure you follow the steps swiftly even as you read.

The following are techniques needed to finish the job:

Weaving

Downhill single Flame Stitch

Wrapping

These techniques are very basic and must have been acquired from the beginning of this book if otherwise, make sure you revise the section that deals with techniques.

Materials:

33 in. 20-gauge dead-soft copper wire

3½ ft. 24-gauge dead-soft copper wire

50mm gemstone donut

10mm large-hole copper bead

3mm bead

40 80 seed beads

Daisy spacer with large hole

Ruler

Chain nose pliers

Round nose pliers

The following are the things to get ready before going to the main work:

Step 1

Weave a bail for a donut-shaped stone with about a large 50mm jasper donut.

Step 2

Make sure that the weave is adjustable to fit any size

Step 3

Prepare the Downhill Single Flame Stitch technique for it would be needed at the woven section.

Step 4

You will need to learn if you have not mastered how to embellish with seed beads for a dash of color and texture.

To the main project now, make sure everything needed —the techniques, materials and the pre-working stages —is ready.

Then follow the step-by-step guide below:

Step 1
Making the base wire. For the base wire, pick a 20-gauge wire and cut six pieces of it. Drop this.

Step 2
Then, pick the 24-guage wire and cut one piece of it for the weaving wire.

Step 3
At this stage, you will need to know how much wire needed for your base stone.

Step 4
Then, Wrap a cord or string through the stone.

Step 5

Make a mark for the overlap.

Step 6

Caution needs to be taken here make sure the measurement of this length is 2½ inches.

Step 7

To complete the overlapping, add 3 in. to that measurement of the length of the base wires.

Step 8

Make a cut of six 5½ in. pieces of wire.

Step 9

Pick up the base wire #6 at the top of the Weave.

Step 10

You will need to string a 60 seed bead about 1 in. from the end of base wire 6.

Step 11

Make sure that this spacer bead makes room in the weave to add more beads later.

Step 12

Pick the weaving wire, now, place it to the right of the bead and on top of the base wire. Make sure the placement is 1 in. from the end.

Step 13

Then, at the center where both wires (base and weaving) overlapped, hold it with your left thumb and index finger.

Step 14

With everything held in the right place and proportion, wrap the weaving wire three times to the right of the bead.

Step 15

You want to prepare the base wires for weaving. Do this by doing the Downhill Wire Preparation.

Step 16

For this Downhill wire preparation, make a single Wrap.

Step 17

On base wire #1, at the bottom of the weave, string a spacer seed bead, and then complete the last wrap of the Downhill Wire Preparation.

Step 18

Remove the two spacer beads to the left and slide them back on base wires #1 and #6 to the right of the weave.

Step 19

Bring the weaving wire from behind up two base wires and go between base wires #4 and #5.

Step 20

Note that this must put you at the top of the hill as you bring the weaving wire up, over, and straight down the back, making the jump behind the weave so you can repeat the downhill pattern.

Step 21

Begin Downhill Flame Stitch Weave single wrap. At the bottom of every hill, at base wire #1, string a seed bead on base wires #1 and #6.

Step 22

You will continue with Downhill Flame Stitch Weave, stringing seed beads on base wires #1 and #6 as you go.

Step 23

Don't panic if your stitches don't want to stay in neat i.e., like in the diagonal lines because you could pinch them with chain nose pliers to make them line up.

Step 24

Now, continue the Downhill Flame Stitch Weave for the length you originally measured with the cord.

Step 25

When the weaving is completed, slide each wire out individually until the weave is centered.

Step 26

Then, wrap the weaving wire three times around base wire #6 and trim the end tightly on the back.

Step 27

You will need to push the weave into the hole of the stone and center the stone.

Step 28

With this, make a U-shaped bend to fit the stone very well. Now, remove the stone.

Step 29

You must have noticed that there are several ends that need to be finished.

Step 30

Because of this, make a 90-degree bend inward with base wires #1 and #6. They should cross each other inside the weave.

Step 31

At this stage, end base wires #2, #4, and #5 straight down on the inside of the weave, over the top of the two crossed wires. Make sure you trim all the three wires to about 3⁄8 in.

Step 32

With the round nose pliers, curl the ends of the three wires over the crossed wires to lock them in place.

Step 33

Trim the two crossed wires close, up against base wires #2 and #5.

Step 34

Repeat steps 9–11 on the other side of the weave. Put the donut back in.

Step 35

Then, with chain nose pliers, pinch the two #3 base wires that are standing straight up.

Step 36

This will bring the two sides in, right up against each other for the next step.

Step 37

Make a double wrap around one of the #3 base wires. It doesn't matter which one, as long as it is tight.

Step 38

Trim the end and pinch it down.

Step 39

On the remaining base wire, string a spacer bead, a 10mm copper bead, and a 3mm bead.

Step 40

Make a Double-Wrapped Loop at the top of these beads. If you are adding a chain as you must have planned, connect the chain to the loop before you complete the wraps.

Your work is now ready. This is a very simple way of making stunning jewelry.

DOUBLE-CROSSED WOVEN BRACELET

This exceptionally beautiful bracelet has a large center focal bead. This project can be a little bit tricky because the woven bezel has two open ends, but you get better with practice.

Materials:
- 19 in. 14-gauge dead soft copper wire
- 7 ft. 20-gauge dead-soft copper wire
- 8 ft. 24-gauge dead-soft copper wire
- 20x25mm cabochon
- 18 80 seed beads

Materials for the Bezel:

- 3 ft. 20-gauge dead-soft copper wire
- 2 ft. 24-gauge dead-soft copper wire

Steps

1. To start with, measure 9 and a half inches piece of your 14 gauge wire and cut. You will need two of this for the outer frame wires. Measure and cut eleven, 7 and a half inches of your 20 gauge wire, these are the base wires. Measure and cut two 3 and a half feet of your 24 gauge wire for the weaving wires. Get your tools in place, and work starts.

2. Pick the 14 gauge base wire, make a wraparound it three times using the end of the weaving wire. Make the wires firm by weaving a double wrap for the six base wires. For this project, the scale weave is employed. It is essential to identify the center wire. To do this, therefore, it becomes easier to identify when you pull out that center wire a little farther than all the other base wires.

3. Pick another new 14 gauge wire, wrap the weaving wire around it three times, do this till you complete the uphill wire preparation using the double wrap for seven base wires.

4. Place the first section above the second and using the top weaving wire, wrap twice around the 7th and 8th base wires. Now the two sections are joined, the snake weave can begin.

5. Starting with the bottom weaving wire, wrap twice around the 6th and 7th base wires. Note that the 7th base wire is the center wire. Continue the double snake weave for eight stitches. Here the weave starts to separate and a diamond-like shape is formed.

6. Pick the top weaving wire that is between the 7th and 8th base wires and weave the flame stitch weave upwards, making double wraps till the top. On the lower section, push the

bottom waving wire down from behind and then pull up between the 4th and 5th base wires. Then wrap twice around the 5th and 6th base wires. Continue this downwards using the flame stitch weave, making double wraps till the bottom.

7. On the other upper half, weave four stitches of double wrap flame stitch downwards. On the lower half, weave upwards using the flame stitch. And wrap around the 6th and 7th base wires twice, with double wraps till the middle.

8. Just as you did when you were joining the two sections together before, bring the top weaving wire down to wrap 7th and 8th base wires twice. Complete the Double Snake Weave for 16 stitches. This is the foundation for the focal stone. Separate the weave as you did in step 5. Make the same diamond shape in the weave. When the two weaving wires

come again together, weave double snake weave for eight stitches.

9. Repeat step 5 to separate both sections. Then wrap 3 times, the weaving wire around the 13th base wire. Trim each of the weaving wire close to the back and pinch downwards. Place the weave on the base wires and complete a crisscross finished end on each end of the bracelet. Be sure to start with one seed bead on the 12th base wire, to stay in place and make up for the odd number of the base wires.

10. On the end of the crisscross sections, make a double wrap loop. Thus part of the piece is finished.

Now! **The double-crossed bezel** is next.

Step 1

Measure and cut two 6inches pieces of 20gauge for the outside base wires. Measure from the 20-gauge wire eight pieces, 3inches each and cut them. Measure and cut two 12 inches of 24 gauge weaving wire.

Step 2

Weave the sides of the bezel. Using a single wrap, measure and cut four 3inches pieces of 24-gauge wire and one 6inches piece. Weave six hills using the flame stitch and single wraps. Once this is done, repeat the whole process while turning it 180 digress to make an identical piece that is a mirror image of the first bezel side.

Step 3

Push both pieces of the bezel into the side of the stone. Use the stone to mold the shape. Crisscross the base wires of each of the bezel piece. Pull the first two base wires down and over the opposite side so that they almost touch the woven part. This indicates where you should make the first loops on the crossed wires. Turn it around and do the same thing on the other side—crisscross the wires and pull the first two down

Step 4

Wrap the first two base wires on each side around the opposite side with a loose loop, and this is to keep the open ends balanced so that the weaving come smooth and fitting. Do not tighten this yet, just wrapped around the edges to hold the bezel intact.

Step 5

With the first two base wires holding the shape, wrap the other base wires around the opposite sides, trim them about 3/8 in., and make a loose loop around the outside base wire. Try not to pull in on the outside base wire and keep the original shape established by the first two base wires.

Step 6

Wrap the ends of the other side as you did the first, taking care to maintain the shape of the bezel. On the back, tighten the loops by trimming them if they are too long and pinching them down. Keep checking the fit by putting the stone back in and molding the wire to the contour.

Step 7

Bend the two long base wires on either side of the bezel straight back at a 45-degree angle. Slide the two base wires inside the diamond pattern with the center wire between them. Do this on both sides. Use a T-pin to make room for the base wires if they don't want to go in there. Put the stone in the bezel and slide it up to the bracelet to secure it.

Step 8

On the back, bend the base wires to the side, go through the 5th base wire of the bezel, and pull it straight down. Don't tighten it yet; leave it a little loose. Do this to all four base wires, so they hold the bezel right up against the bracelet.

Step 9

As you make the loops, check to make sure the bezel is in the center of the bracelet. Tighten the loops underneath when you are sure the bezel is placed where you want it.

Trim the loops and pinch them down to tighten. Trim the base wires and pinch them down.

To conclude,

Step 10

Make a gooseneck hook and attach it as a clasp to the end of the bracelet. Bend the bracelet to fit the hand you want to. Try it on!

Step 11

Create a finish with liver of sulfur and hand buff.

MAKING AND INSTALLING CLASPS

When ending a piece of jewelry, most notably, bracelet, necklace, etc., the clasp is what hold the two ends together. A clasp connects both ends of the piece, allowing you to open and close the piece when putting it on or taking it off while complimenting its beauty. There are quite a number of clasps designs, and this is also subject to creativity and innovation. Many types of clasps are available in the market for purchase, but you make yours. To mention but a few, we have the loop clasps, S-clasp, etc.

In this book, we will be considering how to make a few clasps and also how to install them.

1. **S-Clasp**
   Materials:
   Wire- two pieces of 20 gauge wire of 3cm each
   Round nose pliers
   Mandrel- pen (this is optional)

Steps

a. Measure and cut the stipulated amount of wire. Mark, using a marker, the 1/3 point of the wire both from ends and using a round nose plier, make a curve in the wire at each of this point to form an S shape.

b. With the tip of your round nose plier, make small loops at each ends facing outwards.

c. Now close one side tightly though cautiously. The open side serves as the clasps.

NOTE: To install this S-Clasp on a bracelet or necklace. Attach one side to one loop of the bracelet before closing it tightly. The other side will be left open, and this side gives ease of wearing.

2. The loop clasp
Materials:

Round nose plier

Wire of 5 or 6."

Steps

a. Pick the wire of 5 or 6" and use the round nose plier to bend one of the ends of the wire over to about 1.5" from the end

b. Then, make a loop by wrapping the wire ends around the pliers.

c. Then, to finish the wrapping process, hold the bottom of the pliers and complete it.

d. While making the loop, be very sure that the whole is very large to contain the hook you want to use.

e. Turn and bring the wire around and keep rolling the wire in order to make the loop center over the wire.

f. Hold the loop very well with the pliers and wrap the wire up to two to three times.

g. When the loop is fine in shape, clip close it.

h. Peradventure, the wraps are not close together and take the bent nose pliers and pinch everything up.

i. Turn the clipped end to face you, grab and hold the wire above the wrap.

j. After the grab at length, bend it towards the back

k. At this point, you will need to make the loop like the time you started. Wrap down the first wrap.

l. Now you will need to make a clip very close to the first wrap that you've bent.

m. Then, squeeze smoothly so that the ends of the clip will join together.

This is the end of your clasp. Mind you, there are many things that can be attached to this clasp. In fact, earrings can fit in very well.

LIVER OF SULFUR, POLISHING, AND WAXING OF THE PROJECTS

Liver of Sulfur is, basically, an oxidation agent that is used to add patina to the jewelry created. Basically, LOS is very important because you are dealing with iron and thus, they would surely depreciate with time. LOS, actually, is of two types the gel type and the Lump liver type. The two will as well worn out with time. To create LOS, you will need the following:

For a Lump Liver of Sulfur type:

- Pea-sized lump of LOS
- 1 cup hot (not boiling) distilled water
- 1 cup of cold water
- 1 teaspoon baking soda
- 2 plastic or glass bowls

For the Gel Liver of Sulfur:s
- 1 cup hot (not boiling) distilled water
- 1 cup of cold water
- 1 teaspoon baking soda
- 2 plastic or glass bowls

To apply them you will need to dip a paintbrush to get enough of the Gel and add it gradually as if you were painting.

After getting the LOS, the following are the step-by-step guide to how it can be applied to the projects:

Step 1

You are going to prepare more than one bowl. In the first bowl, pick up the prepared LOS, place it directly in relatively hot water.

Step 2

Immediately, keep at stirring the oxidant agent using rubber to avoid being burnt.

Step 3

When you have stirred consistently, you will notice a yellowish color of the water. For now, you are done with the first bowl.

Step 4

You are ready for the second bowl. There, measure a cup full of cold water not hot.

Step 5

Immediately, pick baking soda of about 55mml, add it and stir too. There won't be a change in the color of the water, though. Making you keep stirring until the particles of the soda dissolved —you can monitor it by checking it through the pestle from time to time.

Step 6

The actual reason for the soda is to render the patina in order to debar it from being too dark in color and maintaining its color.

Step 7

The two contents are ready. Gently repeatedly till the color of the jewelry turns to the color you want, dip the jewelry into the hot water first. Make sure you avoid direct contact with the content; it could be toxic, really.

Step 8

Don't panic if the change in color is not instant; the substance works on jewelry gradually and not instant. This is why you'd need to dip the content continually as you monitor the color.

Step 9

Once the color is as dark as you want it, dip it into the cold content; the second bowl. Basically, the cold water will stop the reaction of the LOS and its constituents like the patina on the jewelry. This is the more reason you must be sure the color has got to what you want before dipping it into the second bowl.

Step 10

Then, take it gently and in a simple way and dry it. Take up a paper towel to enhance the drying.

Step 11

There are varying colors depending on the type of wire you have used. For the three projects, they are basically built with base wire of silver and a copper as the warp wire. The copper wire will be a bit darker than the rest. Other colors from the wires including fine silver, sterling, and others will vary.

Step 12

After the dipping and drying, you will need buffing cloth to clean every angle of the jewelry. The effect of the cleaning is so that the patina will be erased totally and make the brightness of the jewelry to be pronounced.

Step 13

Make sure you clean from every space and within the weave so that the patina will leave all the angles of the jewelry.

Step 14

Should it not be bright as you have envisaged, repeat the cleaning process. You can use a clean cloth to hold it as you finish up the cleaning.

Caution

You have to prepare as the thickness of the wire will determine how thorough you will clean the jewelry. The oxidation in copper will be removed quickly than other types of wires, be prepared. Don't at any point have contact with the LOS; it could affect your skin.

POLISHING

Polishing of wire is simply making it brighter. It is an essential part of the jewelry making as they are the latter part that brings out the quality of the work –it can't be neglected. You must be careful with cleaning as it is totally different from polishing. There are different ways you can use to polish your projects as discussed before. Two of these ways include:

Using the hand polishing

The basic thing that you need is a red rouge and a cloth. It is one of the basic technique. You add the rouge on the cloth and clean the jewelry gently. Amazingly, you can do this even before building the work but only make sure you keep the cloth for onward cleaning after the conclusion. After that, you will need the toothpaste now. Add it to the cloth and clean gently. The color of the wires should be shining amazingly now. With warm water, rinse the red rouge off the jewelry. This is one of the cheapest methods because you don't need to buy any special thing. However, you can buy cloth special made for jewelry because it is in-built with red rouge. The work is ready.

Using the Ionic cleaner

This is one of the fastest jewelry polishing technique. Though it could be expensive because of the materials needed, it is one of the safest of all. It works in a special way as the gemstone, such as the one in the earring of the project, does not get broken in the cleaning process. You will apply it gently and make sure it flows in between the wire, especially for the woven wires. After it had got to the corners, pull it out everything. This is all for the technique. Clean it all totally, and the work is ready.

WAXING

This is another special way of preparing the jewelry for usage. Waxing basically prevents the wires from rust. This is done by helping it to maintain its color throughout the usage. This is one of the oldest forms of wire preservation. The steps of applying wax or waxing of the three projects discussed in this book are very necessary. It is pertinent to note that as the processes of preserving wires and enhancing the beauty of jewelry have been discussed, they can be applied in their chronological order. That is, LOS, Polishing, and Waxing can be applied to the same jewelry at different times for the same purpose. To wax, follow these steps:

Step 1

Prepare the jewelry for waxing by using a buff cloth to clean the surface. Make sure every point of the weave is cleansed of dust.

Step 2

Pick the alcohol content and add it to a different cloth until it is saturated with enough to clean off once the jewelry.

Step 3

Rub the cloth gently on the jewelry round and at every hidden point of the weave.

Step 4

Apply the coating of the wire to polish it round and softly.

Step 5

Leave the jewelry to dry and expose it only to humidity; avoid direct sunlight contact. The beauty is coming showing up already. Let the polish dry off very well.

Step 6

You will need to buff the jewelry now. This can be done using a machine such as a stockinette roll. However, you can use a wool-like cloth to clean gently. If perhaps what you are doing has a quite large surface and are many, use the electric drill to make the work easier and faster.

Step 7

After you have done everything, your work is ready. However, try to repeat the processes again to get the desired results. This is because the waxing might not be obvious really at the first application; the effect is most obvious when the process is repeated.

Every one of the projects is more or less incomplete without proper application of the LOS, polish, and wax respectively. Take note of everything and use your jewelry.

In conclusion, take every one of the additional effects suggested as an advantage to beautify your works. They will give your works the desired professionality, stunning look, and charming usage that will fit very well to your clients desired.

CRAFT WIRE VS. 0.999 FINE SILVER

While making pieces of jewelry using wires, understanding the texture and nature of the wires used is very important. Of this reason is why understanding craft wire and 0.999 fine silver nature is paramount. A craft wire ranges in its softness. A 0.999 fine silver has been a huge source of investment because of its purity and quality. These two wires are commonly used in jewelry making to ensure the sustenance of the work. Though the two wires are very flexible compared to other types of wires, they serve different purposes. This is because craft wires are always very suitable for the base and the fine silver for warp wire.

The size of the wires has been the contributing factor for their difference. Craft wires are between the 16 to 24 gauge and Fine silver ranges from 4 to any length depending on the project at hand. They are very flexible and body friendly. As the base wire, craft wire is very effective because the texture is soft, cool and accommodating for wires to weave on.

The 0.999 fine silver, which also refers to as the three nines, is very good for making curves and bends in jewelry making. The level of its purity is what makes it to be referred to as the .999. It is used because it is coated with silver and thus, durable for long time usage.

The length of craft wire and fine silver are different; they are determined by what the user wants. In their length, one could get different colors tinted around for a suitable bracelet or necklace. For the purity suitable for jewelry making, use the 92.5 percent stamped level of fine silver. The range in level of purity is not applicable to a craft wire.

The two wires are good for jewelry because, in the technique of wire works, there are different bending, cutting, buffing, pulling, etc. which will not be good for just random wires. With these wires, you are sure of durability and amazing friendly usage. The two wires are very easy to manipulate round during works; regardless of the technique, they work effectively.

Whatever the scenario, craft wires are good for base wires, especially in the weaving technique, while fine silver will always be the warp. Warps are always the most noticeable part of jewelry, and because fine silver comes with different colors, you are sure things will be in place without special polishing.

HOW TO SPLICE ON MORE WIRE IF YOU RUN OUT

As a wire weaving jewelry maker, most especially beginner, running out of wire is what happens. This is because a change in wire sizes, inaccurate size estimation, type of wire, and lots more, will affect the end product of the work. Experts might know their way around the scenario, even though it might not be perfect. There are different things to be done but there are few basic things that could give a fast and accurate result. Though splicing, as part of the techniques, has been discussed earlier, understanding how it can be used for manipulation is a special case –why this section is a necessity. As a beginner, you were working and suddenly exhaust your wire, don't panic. The following processes explain how to splice on more wire if you run out. If you are to work towards a finished piece and you are going to do a big long weave. You are going to learn how to end a wire and add a wire if you run out.

Actually, there are two basic things to do while splicing wire: either you run out of wire because you want to start new weave or you run out of wire because you want to end the work.

Note that the steps given here can fit into any of the techniques you are using. In other words, you are the determiner of when to incorporate splicing of the wire. However, no matter the situation, you will always need to end a wire; this is why it is important to know how to splice wire when you run out of it.

TO END A WIRE

Step 1

Once you are at the end of the wire, you need to trim it.

Step 2

Be careful not to trim anyhow because you have a choice of when to trim it. Then take the pointy flush cutter and trim.

Step 3

Observe the wideness of the point you are, do not trim it when it is doing a wide weave. Therefore, hold all the warp wire tight to its base as you trim.

Step 4

Because if you clip the warp wire at the point of wide weave, it could pull out and it would be like a weave that goes up and swing over the wrap wire itself, move away from the wide point. You can reduce the wire backwards to a tight point since you can't continue.

Step 5

Still at the point of trim, you should trim it when it is in a nice tight coil because it has a little knot or acts like a little knot.

Step 6

Move the last coil of the pattern of the weave wire and trim really tight in between the two wrap wires.

Step 7

Trim between the two wrap wires so the tail sat in between. In there, they are nice and safe and will not catch on anything –such as piercing and damaging the skin, damaging clothes, and many more.

Step 8

At this point, you will notice that the trim is on one coil instead of having it at the end of the second coil. This is because at that point, you can come into the new wire and build the second wire coil at the bottom of the warp wire and then continue so it won't disrupt the flow.

You have to be careful not to leave the tight wires loosed and you might need to start from the beginning. More so, you have to be careful in the process of trimming to not let the warp and the base wires bend.

Step 9

To trim the weave wire, use your pointy flush cutter which will not only allow just the tip on the wire but also let you continue with the coil and weaves.

Step 10

Once you are at a significant distance away from the start of the new wire, you trim the weave start too by trimming it allowing it to sit in between the base wire. Therefore, it is essential you have a very pointy flush cutter.

Caution

Make sure the tail ends are hidden and wouldn't catch on anything. If peradventure you cut it too long, you can trim it again or you could use your chain nose pliers burnish it. The goal is to keep it (the tail) as invisible as possible.

STARTING A NEW WIRE

Adding a new wire is more or less like ending the warp wire (the weaving or adds-on wire). This because the end of the wire is the beginning of the other. Both processes work hand-in-hand; where one ends, the other is expected. The ending of a wire does not necessarily mean you have completed the job, but rather you can suggest the adding of new wire because the other ran out. The following are practical steps to starting a new wire:

Step 1

At the point where you finished your wire, pick a wire of same size and more length. The length is required to avoid the end of the wire. Make sure you straighten the new wire to avoid the rumpling –make it ready for usage.

Note that you must have kept the wires tight together before sorting for the new one.

Step 2

At this point of inserting the wire, check the gap whether it is wide. If it is intact, pull the finished wire to the back and insert the new one from the front.

Step 3

You will need to hold the finished warp wire tightly and with that tightness, insert the new one and continue the weaving.

Step 4

After the weaving has got to a reasonable length, check the point and make sure there is no disparity in the wires, even in the patterns. If otherwise, try to adjust the new wire holding the finished one tight.

Step 5

With the wire intact, trim the two wires together. The wires should be of equal length and not be able to catch on things around it; it could even injure you.

The addition is ready. Incorporate these tricks at every point of your work. Many people say using joining at the point of weaving creates an outstanding effect; this will not be true to you until you try it out. Good luck!

INCORPORATION OF BEADS INTO DESIGNS

At the points and stages of jewelry designs lie the incorporation of beads. Whatever the kind of technique in use, incorporating beads into the design is very easy and done in a simple way.

Step 1

When you get to String a 60 seed bead on each outside of a 20-gauge base wire.

Step 2

The beads must be given in even spacing and add color.

Step 3

Pick the beads and thrust the wires through. Then repeat the crossing of the next two wires in the center.

Step 4

Bend them to the back, trim, and loop them next to the bead on the outside 20-gauge base wires.

Step 5

Continue to make a pyramid of beads and crossed wires.

Step 6

Trim and tighten each loop when it is in place. The outside 20-gauge wires should cross at the top.

Step 7

Using flat nose pliers, bend in the outside framing wires to echo the angle of the bead pyramid.

Step 8

Cross them at the top, right over left.

Step 9

Wrap the 20-gauge wires around the 14-gauge framing wires twice. Trim the end and pinch tightly.

In another way, you can work with different works than the earrings.

When the jewelry is bracelet, necklace or any other thing, consider using the following steps:

Step 1

Measure and cut a 24-gauge wire to your desired length.

Step 2

At the tip of the round nose pliers, pinch the wire at the center and pull the ends using the plier itself. While making the pull, be sure it results in a small loop. So, the pulling must be in opposite directions.

Step 3

Drop the first loop made, measure and cut three pieces of 20-gauge for base wires.

Step 4

One after the other, pick the base and string the beads you have prepared there until the height of the stringed-beads gets to 1 inch. Repeat this for all the base wires.

Step 5

Then place the first base and the third on the right and left sides respectively.

Step 6

Then, hold the wires with your thumb and slide the small loop created in step 1 to the base wire 2.

Step 7

Put the ends of the wires of the first and third under the warp wire.

Step 8

Then, move the warp wire from the top and take it over the third base wire but very close to the loop and betwixt base wires one and two.

Step 9

With the same wire put in proper bend the beads by moving straight and at the back of the bundle of the wires.

Step 10

Then, move the warp wire from the below over but betwixt base wires two and three. Be careful to ensure that the place to make good bend is opened by making the warp wire very close to the seed beads.

Step 11

At the base wire 2 as well, slide a bead there.

Step 12

As you've done before, take the warp wire betwixt and over the base wires one and two. Maintain the kind of pattern you have created from the beginning.

Step 13

Pick the wire and pull it towards the back to make a bend.

Step 14

Then, pick the warp from below, and take it over the bundle and put it betwixt base wires two and three.

Step 15

Don't drop the wire yet, take it to the back to make a bend.

The work is ready. Make sure you move towards the kind of jewelry you are making. Repeating the steps might be the best option.

HELPFUL TIPS FOR WIRE WEAVING

1. Learn to improvise: You do not, necessarily, need to buy expensive tools for every jewelry project and work. Basic household objects can be used, sometimes. Use household objects for shaping jewelry. For example, you can use a round barreled pencil or pen to straighten your wire. You can do this by placing the wire between your thumb and the pen then pull the wire through several times. Bottles can make bracelets' mandrels, just be careful not to hammer them.

2. Keep your weaves kink-free: If due to a mistake you need to unwrap a section of the weave, be sure to straighten and smoothen out that section before you continue weaving. To avoid breakage, make sure your weave is kink-free. And if there is a link, straighten it out right away. A kink is a potential weak point that can lead to a break.

3. Your hands, your best tool: As much as possible, resist from always grabbing a tool to do all of your work. Your hands can do it better. Appreciate your best tool but remember to take breaks and stretch your hands as often as possible too.

4. Create a buffer between your fingers and the wire: Create a buffer using a pliable fabric tape so as to reduce the friction between your fingers directly against the wire. Letting the wire move constantly over your fingers can cause an injury or wear due to heat from friction.

5. Keep your base wire evenly spaced: it is not easy to do, but it is important to keep an equal distance between the base wires. When weaving, you can space the point at which you're weaving till about half an inch then allow it spread and flare out to allow you weave easily. If holding onto the wire with your hands is not working so well yet, make use of a wooden ring clamp. It secures all the wires in place without marking them. With just the strength of your fingers, the wires are held in place.

6. Make them tight and fitted: Pull the weaving wire tightly against each frame wire with every wrap. Make sure the weaving wire lies perfectly flat when it travels across two frame wires. Push the weaves together too! Tension is necessary when weaving. If your weaves are too tight, you will pull your base wires out of shape. But leaving it loose, you have uneven spacing between your wrap wires.

7. Round-nose pliers can be used as mandrels: Round-nose pliers can be used to create loops before shaping the wire further. To form a loop, position the round-nose pliers where you would like to make a large loop, leaving the round-nose pliers open. Grip the end of the wire with your fingers and wrap the wire around the jaw of the round-nose pliers. Remove the pliers and continue to shape the rest of the wire with your finger.

8. A sampler is of great importance: Deciding on which weave to use for a project can be tasking and confusing. So to help you get started on a wire weaving project, make a sampler. Make all different weave styles and make sure each has a loop (on the folded side). With the loop, attach the weaves to a safety pin. This is to give you easy access and this way you would not lose any.

9. Make sure the maintenance of all your equipment is always done at stipulated and continuous times. This means that every iron part of the equipment like pliers will need oil at every point to prevent it from rusting.

SKILL BUILDING EXERCISES

While doing some of the techniques most especially the weaving and wrapping, you must have noticed the pains you sustained. Also, while using the cutter and the pliers —in fact the equipment —you will or might sustain some injuries too. Additionally, doing the skills might be awkward at times because you are not used to them —this is normal. These and other reasons necessitated this section. Therefore, in this section, there will be suggested skill-building exercises that would help you make your hand flexible, reduce pains after long work, and many other things that might be an object of challenge through wire weaving works. These building exercises include:

Stringing large-hole items

This involves stringing something on a large-hole with an ending. You could enhance and make free your hands by just picking up a tough wire and create a large-hole (loop). With the loop, begin the stringing of the wires together till you achieve a considerable length even though you couldn't finish the dead ends. Don't forget that refining the motor skills is what you attain with consistent practice of this exercise.

Stringing smaller beads

Likewise, you could be able to string small beads even with the large holes like the first exercise given. To start, use a yarn with finished ends, perhaps with a tape or a plastic lacing and wrap to a large loop. With this exercise, you can get more effective with the way you swing your hand while weaving. In fact, you can get complex painting pasta and or creating paper beads.

Making a friendship bracelet

With this exercise, you could get on the original jewelry; bracelet. Working with the bracelet for improvement, you will make it personal in the sense that bigger bracelet can be reduced —and smaller ones too —to your size. Here as well, you will need to practice painting the bracelet to the color that you want never buy paints without a proper guide. Like the processing of adding LOS, you can polish the bracelet just to get you much more ready even for subsequent works. While you are not really creating a novel work, your painting, coloring, polishing, etc. skills are enhanced.

Adding buttons to a bracelet

You can pick a common bracelet which could enable stringing buttons to it and get on it. Make sure you are using the basic technique while adding thee buttons. In fact, this exercise is sportive as every button added could create a great sensation, even for a novel pattern. This is an exercise that would increase your skill of using button and clasp while making jewelry. You could make it a style that at every bracelet you made, there will be enough button to stunt the style.

Making incessant loops and earrings connection

This exercise is recommended because while making earring connection with loops, it is very difficult to maintain the wires held together. The skill that will enhance is gripping alongside holding within a given range, the wires while making loops and even earrings connection. This will make you more creative, smart and intelligent in handling wires to connect earrings. The project on earrings is the best example for you to notice the point where you could practice this skill. You could proceed with seashell earrings and flower necklace because many of them are crafted with lots of sewing skills that will enable your creativity, especially your connection of earrings.

Using only 1 wire

With just a single wire, you could fold it and make weaving for a considerable long time. While this might not fetch you all the skills, you will understand the texture of your wire and the best way to handle them. If you understand your wire, you will know how to and when to buy your wires for work. Apart from this, there will be lots of technique to practice while starting or ending a wire. This is very effective during leisure time. There is no time to be checking for wires in a special way, most times when you have a good number of works to do. This is very much effective for everyone. In fact, you could wrap the wire in whatever way you like it. Loose the wire and repeat the same thing you are doing until you achieve.

Swinging wires with different sizes

This exercise is done by simply swinging wires around one another for a good number of times. Make sure you have wires of different sizes and shape so that weaving speed will increase, even with accuracy. This does not really suggest just rolling wires without making the wires straighten, rather, dwindling the wires at different but specific directions. This will enhance your weaving skill. Likewise, the hand flexibility will be there at any point you are while doing the wire works. This is not specific to some techniques, but general to every point.

Rounding off this section, the exercises that would improve your skills could be personal. Therefore, you might need to understand the problem you are facing. To say, differences in human and their perception coupled with strength will be of greater consideration while selecting exercises; especially effective ones at that. For instance, a southpaw will surely follow different directions at weaving, overlapping, and moving round the wires –compared to a right-handed person. The bottom line is that while taking these exercises will do lots, understanding perfectly who you are and your strength will do much more.

In conclusion, these skills are suggested to improve your moving and handling of the wires to achieve the best and desired results.

METRIC CONVERSION CHART

Length Conversion Table of Common Length Units

	Milli meter (mm)	Centi meter (cm)	Meter (m)	Kilom eter (km)	Inch (in)	Foot/ feet (ft)	Yard (yd)
1 milli mete r (mm)	1	0.1	0.001	0.000 001	0.3937 007874 0157	0.003 28083 98950 131	0.001 0936 1329 8337 7
1 centi mete r (cm)	10	1	0.01	0.000 01	0.3937 007874 0157	0.032 80839 89501 31	0.010 9361 3298 3377
1 mete r (m)	1000	100	1	0.001	39.370 078740 157	3.280 83989 50131	1.093 6132 9833 77
1 kilo mete r (km)	10000 00	1000 00	1000	1	39370. 078740 157	3280. 83989 50131	1093. 6132 9833 77
1 inch (in)	25.4	2.54	0.025 4	0.000 0254	1	0.083 33333	0.027 7777

						33333 33	7777 7778
1 foot / feet (ft)	304.8	30.48	0.304 8	0.000 3048	12	1	0.333 3333 3333 333
1 yard (yd)	914.4	91.44	0.914 4	0.000 9144	36	3	1

Wire conversion Chart

Gauge	Inches	Millimeters
10	0.102	2.59
11	0.091	2.31
12	0.081	2.06
13	0.072	1.83
14	0.064	1.63
15	0.057	1.45
16	0.052	1.29
17	0.0045	1.14
18	0.04	1.02
19	0.0036	0.91
20	0.032	0.81
21	0.028	0.71
22	0.025	0.64
23	0.023	0.58
24	0.02	0.51
25	0.0179	0.455
26	0.0159	0.404
27	0.0142	0.361
28	0.0126	0.32

29	0.0113	0.287
30	0.01	0.25
31	0.0089	0.226
32	0.008	0.2
33	0.0071	0.18
34	0.0063	0.16
35	0.0056	0.142
36	0.005	0.13
37	0.0045	0.114
38	0.004	0.1

The conversation given here is strictly on the measurement used throughout the book. Apply your calculation using a calculator where necessary. Note that while measuring the wires, the centimeter and millimeter gauge of the wire could be used too with a ruler.

CONCLUSION

In conclusion, wire work is one of the most domesticated but lucrative skills that can be done by anyone at any point in time. This is because it requires only some basic techniques and readily available materials. In this book, we have exhaustively explained all you need to know about wire weaving.

The techniques discussed are very simple to apply. There is no need for prior knowledge as this book is for beginners; though it takes into consideration every level of knowledge in wire works. The step by step guide on the techniques in the book makes everything easier and beautiful.

Anyone who wants a job on wire works, even outside the ones discussed here, will need the knowledge of this book. Amazingly, it is like a glance of only cogent information of jewelry making. It is advisable to, for effectiveness sake, work as you read. With this, the total utility and intention of this book will be fulfilled.

Over time, there had barely been, according to statistics of jewelry making through wire works, a book that is summary in nature but very useful for everyone. This book is solely for business if you know what that means.

Before reading the bulky part of this book, read the materials section in order to get them ready. Don't panic; you will be taken through the journey of wire works. Stay glued to knowledge!

HELPFUL LINKS TO LEARN MORE

https://www.beaducation.com

 https://www.youtube.com/wireworks

https://www.jewelrymaking.about.com/od/wiretech niquesinfo/ss/052608.htm

https://www.youtube.com/watch?v=lfy3mLLAMIE

https://www.studiodax.wordpress.com/2011/01/16/i -heart-hearts/

https://www.jewellrymakingjournal.com/wire- wrap-rings-tutorial/

https://www.goodconverters.com

https://www.firemoutaingems.com

https://www.youtube.com/watch?v=s9mSfXyeTOY

Made in the USA
Lexington, KY
14 August 2019